teeny tiny
gardening

teeny tiny
gardening

35 step-by-step projects and inspirational ideas
for gardening in tiny spaces

Emma Hardy

CICO BOOKS
LONDON NEW YORK

Published in 2013 by CICO Books
An imprint of Ryland Peters & Small Ltd
519 Broadway, 5th floor, New York NY 10012
20–21 Jockey's Fields, London WC1R 4BW

www.cicobooks.com

10 9 8 7 6 5 4 3 2 1

A CIP catalog record for this book is
available from the Library of Congress and
the British Library.

ISBN 978 1 908862 80 8

Printed in China

Editor: Caroline West
Designer: Geoff Borin
Photographer: Debbie Patterson
Illustrator: Jane Smith

For digital editions, visit
www.cicobooks.com/apps.php

contents

introduction

Teeny tiny containers are a great way to garden when you are short of space or simply enjoy gardening on a small scale. The idea behind this book is to create gardens in small spaces (both inside and out), using a range of different containers and a wide variety of gorgeous plants. Whether you want to create a short-lived garden for a special occasion or a more productive and fruitful display, you will find lots of ideas here. From vegetables grown in an old wooden crate and fruit in a vintage enamel bread bin to a fun dinosaur garden for children and adorable little succulents in glass tumblers, there are lots of suggestions for gardening in miniature.

Each project includes a materials list and simple step-by-step instructions. I have also included a list of the plants used in each project, which can be followed closely or simply used for inspiration. A visit to your local garden center should provide you with all that you need, with on-line gardening stores making more specialist plants readily available.

I recommend using soil-less potting mix for most of the projects unless something more specific is required—you are probably unlikely to want to invest in a range of different potting media if you are gardening on a small scale. As you gain experience (and possibly more space!), you may want to experiment with more in-depth soil mixtures, but a good-quality, soil-less potting mix should be fine for small, and often temporary, gardens. A few gardening tools will also come in handy, and it is worth investing in some good-quality basics. A decent garden trowel, a good pair of hand pruners (secateurs), and a watering can with a fine rose will all prove useful.

Before you start, it may be helpful to read through the Basic Techniques section (see pages 8–11), which explains some of the terms used in the book and offers advice and information on containers and materials. Look around for interesting and unusual containers, recycling and salvaging where you can, and think about using things around you in different and eye-catching ways.

I hope that you will find lots of ideas in this book for creating some lovely gardening projects and also gain inspiration to help you design and make your own miniature gardens.

basic techniques

Gardening on a teeny tiny scale requires very few special techniques, but these pages offer general advice and information, plus explanations of some of the gardening terms used in the projects that follow.

Choosing containers and plants

All sorts of containers can be used to create sweet little gardens, including teacups, old wooden drawers, and enamel bowls. The most important requirement is that the container has at least one hole in the bottom for drainage or is made from a material that can be punctured to create drainage holes. If you can't make holes in the base of the container, then it will be more suitable for an indoor garden where you can monitor the watering carefully and make adjustments as necessary.

As you are gardening on a tiny scale, it's a good idea to think carefully about the type of plants you are going to grow. For instance, you may wish to look out for dwarf, miniature, or compact varieties of plants such as alpines, dwarf bulbs, and patio roses or opt for slow-growing plants like conifers (as in the evergreen Topiary Garden on pages 84–85).

Preparing pots and plants

Once you have decided on the container that you would like to plant up, you'll need to prepare both the pots and plants before planting. Some of the key tasks include:

• **Making drainage holes** Few plants (apart from bog and water plants) like to sit in very wet soil, so it is important to provide adequate drainage in each container. If the container you are using does not have drainage holes in the bottom, then you can make some by drilling or hammering a heavy-duty nail into the base a few times.

• **Using drainage crocks** These are bits of old plant pot or tiles that are placed over the drainage holes in the container so that the hole will not become blocked by potting mix and inhibit drainage. Simply break up old pots or tiles with a hammer (take care not to let small shards hit you) and keep them for use in future projects.

• **Getting the container ready** To reduce the likelihood of infection by pests and diseases, clean the container on both the outside and inside with warm, soapy water before planting up. Remember to rinse thoroughly.

• **Loosening plant roots** Sometimes plants can become root-bound if they have been sitting in their plastic pots for a long time. Loosening the roots slightly will encourage them to spread out and grow when you re-pot them. Gently press your fingertips into the roots and then tease them out slightly, making sure that you do not damage them as you do so.

• **Soaking plants before planting** Before re-potting a plant, always soak it in water for at least 10 minutes to get the potting mix really wet.

top left *A plastic liner will help to conserve moisture in a container, but cut a few holes in it for drainage.*

Choosing potting mixes

There are two main types of potting mix (also sometimes known as potting compost): soil-based and soil-less (usually either peat- or peat-substitute-based). Soil-based potting mix is a good, all-round mix that provides container plants with adequate food for the first few weeks after planting and is also free-draining, which encourages good root growth. It retains moisture well, but is also less prone to water-logging. Garden centers stock a variety of different soil-based potting mixes suitable for a range of plants, as follows:

• **Seeds and cuttings** A potting mix specifically for growing seeds and cuttings is sterile and light, with a low-nutrient content. It is ideal for giving young seedlings a good start.

• **Annuals and perennials** A richer potting mix with a high-nutrient content is needed to encourage root and foliar growth. It is also moisture-retentive. Specialist bulb potting mix, containing grit or sand, is also available. This is free-draining and provides the ideal environment for growing bulbs.

• **Permanent planting** Plants grown permanently in containers need a nutrient-rich potting mix that contains slow-release fertilizers and will provide them with adequate drainage.

• **Specialist potting mixes** These are available for specific plants, providing them with precise conditions, including cactus potting mix that is very gritty and free-draining; potting mix for roses that has just the right pH levels; and special aquatic potting mix for ponds and water gardens (although this is not needed for the Lush Water Garden project on pages 102–103).

A good soil-based potting mix is essential when container gardening. Buy the best that you can afford and you will be rewarded with strong, healthy plants. Alternatively, you can also make your own using material from a garden compost heap or wormery, but bear in mind that these will not be suitable for growing plants from seed—for these, store-bought sterilized potting mix should be used.

Soil-less potting mix is the other main type of commercially available mix. It contains peat or a peat substitute, and is much lighter and often cheaper than soil-based potting mix. However, it does tend to dry out quickly and the plants will need regular feeding to keep the nutrient levels up. If you are using this type of potting mix, avoid ones that contain peat if possible, as this is now considered environmentally unsound. Soil-less potting mix is absolutely fine for short-term container gardening, but a soil-based potting mix is preferable for container gardening in the long term.

above *Invest in a good-quality potting mix to keep your plants healthy. Choosing specialist potting mixes for plants that require particular nutrients will give the plants the best start.*

Using additives

Horticultural grit and sand can be added to the potting mix to improve drainage and general performance. Note that it is best to use sand rather than grit for small plants that have fine root systems. Grit and sand are needed to grow cacti, succulents, and alpines (which prefer very free-draining conditions) in particular. Vermiculite (a beige or gray expanded mineral) and perlite (a lightweight, white volcanic glass which occurs naturally) will also both improve drainage and aeration, and are readily available from garden centers. While these are not essential, they are helpful in containers.

Mulches and decorative trims

A mulch is a material that covers the top of the potting mix, either to help keep moisture in or simply as a decorative finishing touch. Gravel, for example, helps to keep leaves off the surface of the potting mix and is especially useful around succulents and cacti. Gravel is available in a range of different sizes and colors from garden centers and online. Slate, pebbles, stone and marble chippings, miniature shells, sand, and broken glass pieces can also all be used to add a pretty top-dressing to a pot or container, and are available in a wealth of sizes and colors.

Aftercare

Once you have planted up your container and the new plants are growing nicely, you'll then need to pay some attention to various care and maintenance tasks in order to keep

your tiny garden looking its best, just as you would in the main garden or for larger containers. The most important of these tasks are as follows:

• **Watering** The amount of water plants need varies enormously. Generally, plants will need more water during their growing season. Plants grown in containers will also dry out quickly— certainly more quickly than they would if grown in the open garden. Also, the smaller the container, the more often it will need watering. Aim to keep the potting mix just moist, watering once a day in summer and twice a day in hot weather. On very hot days, you may need to move your containers to a shady spot. The ideal time to water is in the evening rather than in the morning because less water is lost through evaporation at this time of day. Keep an eye on the potting mix in a container and alter your watering routine if the plant starts to look unhappy. Remember that plants grown in terrariums, for example, will need misting occasionally using a water spray bottle.

You can also buy water-retaining granules from garden centers. Although not essential, they can be a useful way of conserving moisture in a small container that would otherwise dry out quickly. Add the granules to the potting mix and stir in well before planting.

If a plant really dries out, plunge the plant (still in its pot) into a sink or bucket of water so that the top of the potting mix is just covered with water. Try to keep the leaves out of the water and weigh the pot down under the water if necessary. Keep the pot submerged for at least half an hour to soak it thoroughly. Take the pot out of the water and leave to drain. The plant should recover within a few hours.

• **Supplementary feeding** There are plenty of fertilizers and plant food mixtures available, some for specific plants (such as roses and tomatoes) and others for more general use. Slow-release general-purpose fertilizers can be added to the potting mix in the container when planting up or gently worked into the surface of the mix after planting with a hand fork. Alternatively, you can feed the plants regularly (either weekly or fortnightly) with a diluted liquid general-purpose fertilizer throughout the growing season (according to the manufacturer's instructions). Another economical option is to invest in a wormery, which will provide fantastic potting mix and also a liquid feed that makes a great fertilizer if you can bear the smell.

If a plant is in need of a quick boost, spray it with a foliar feed, which is a diluted liquid fertilizer sprayed directly onto the plant. This will perk the plant up quickly, although it is not a substitute for feeding the potting mix. Make sure that the plant is sprayed out of full sunlight, so that the leaves will not be damaged.

• **Deadheading** This is a term for cutting or picking off the faded flowers (and also leaves) from a plant to keep the plant tidy and also to encourage the plant to put its energy into producing new flowers rather than setting seed. Deadhead plants every couple of days in order to encourage new growth. You can remove dead flowers by hand from plants with thin stems or use scissors or hand pruners (secateurs) for plants with woodier stems. Not only does deadheading encourage a further flush of flowers, but it can also help to reduce infestations of pests and diseases which can accumulate in dead flowers and leaves.

Dealing with pests and diseases

To reduce the risk of pests and diseases spoiling your beautiful little gardens, follow a few simple rules:

• Make sure that containers are clean and dry before you start planting.

• Always buy healthy plants, avoiding any that look discolored or weak, and check the rootball by pulling the plant out of its pot to make sure that it is pest-free and not too root-bound.

• Make sure plants are potted up in the right potting mix and in a suitable spot. This encourages healthy growth, which in turn reduces the risk of plants succumbing to pests and diseases.

• Check the plants regularly for any signs of infestation.

Aphids (greenfly and blackfly) are common pests that suck the sap from plants and need to be removed as soon as you see them. Commercial treatments are available, but spraying with a dilute solution of water and dish-washing detergent can be effective. Removing aphids by gently wiping them off the plant can prevent infestations, although you'll need to remain vigilant! *Botrytis* (gray mold), a fungal infection, is a common problem which occurs if conditions are damp and ventilation is insufficient. A quickly spreading, gray, dusty mold appears on leaves and stems. Improve air circulation and spray with an organic fungicide if need be. Although proprietary pesticides,

left *Deadhead roses by cutting off the flowerhead just above a leaf joint. This will encourage the rose to continue flowering as well as neaten it up.*

insecticides, and fungicides are available, try to garden organically and avoid chemical-based treatments. Tackling pests or diseases quickly is imperative and can often avoid the need for store-bought solutions.

Useful tools and equipment

Here are some suggestions for the various tools and other pieces of equipment that you'll find useful when gardening on a small scale. This list is by no means exhaustive and does not include more specialized items, which are listed under the specific projects.

Garden trowel

Gardening gloves

Hammer and heavy-duty nail (for putting in drainage holes)

Hand fork

Hand pruners (secateurs)

Plant labels

Scissors

Scoop

Small watering can (with a fine rose)

Tablespoon

Teaspoon

Water spray bottle

bright & beautiful

eggshell gardens

Create an eggshell garden with pastel-colored eggs filled with miniature violas, forget-me-nots, and moss. Choose plants with small roots and check the potting mix, watering regularly to keep your tabletop garden looking good. These gardens are so quick to make that you can simply change the plants when they fade.

materials

Knife

Eggs

Pin

Potting mix (sieved if necessary)

Moss (available from florists)

Egg holder or vintage egg cups

Plants:

Myosotis sylvatica
(forget-me-not)

Selaginella kraussiana
(Krauss' spikemoss)

Viola 'Moonlight' (violet)

Viola odorata (sweet violet)

1 Using the knife, cut the top off each of the eggs, pour out the contents, and rinse thoroughly. Make a few small holes in the bottom of the eggs with the pin, for drainage. Spoon a little potting mix into each egg, making sure that there will be enough room for the plants.

2 Put one plant in each egg and add a little more potting mix if necessary. Push a small piece of moss onto the top of the potting mix if you wish. Group the eggs in an egg holder or display them individually in vintage egg cups to brighten up your table. Deadhead the violas as required, and they'll continue flowering for a few more weeks.

dainty teacups

Collect vintage cups and saucers, and create a pretty desktop garden to brighten up your day. If you are feeling brave, drill a drainage hole in the base of each cup using a hand drill. If you would rather not damage your cups, then adding gravel and being careful not to overwater should keep the plants healthy.

materials

Fine gravel

Teacups and saucers

Potting mix with a little fine gravel added

Selection of alpine plants such as:

Armeria juniperifolia (thrift) in white cup with ornate pattern

Clematis marmoraria in pink cup

Eranthis cilicica (winter aconite) in white cup with blue interior

Fritillaria uva-vulpis (fritillary) in turquoise with gold cup

Primula marginata Dwarf Form (primrose) in white cup with flower

Saxifraga 'Penelope' (saxifrage) in yellow cup with the decorated saucer

Saxifraga × *petraschii* (saxifrage) in gray cup with white flower

Sedum species (stonecrop) in the yellow and gold cup

1 Put about a tablespoon of fine gravel in the bottom of each of the teacups.

2 Spoon some potting mix into the first cup, remembering to leave enough room for the plant.

tip:

Choose alpines or small-scale plants for your teacups. Alternatively, plant small bulbs, such as snowdrops, dwarf narcissi, or grape hyacinths, in the winter so that you will have a pretty floral display in spring.

3 Take the plant out of its plastic pot and gently shake off any excess potting mix. Position the plant in the cup and fill round the edges with more potting mix so that the plant sits firmly in place. Plant the remaining teacups in the same way.

4 Sprinkle some fine gravel over the surface of the potting mix in each cup, making sure that it is completely covered. Water each cup carefully, ensuring that the mix is damp but not waterlogged. Deadhead spent flowers as necessary, to keep the plants in bloom.

spring garden basket

Create a spring garden in a basket by choosing beautiful paperwhite narcissi for their delicious fragrance and mixing them with grape hyacinths, primulas, and pansies. Lining the basket with moss adds a woodland feel. The moss will need to be kept moist to retain its color, so mist with a water spray bottle.

materials

Wire basket

Moss (available from florists)

Green or black plastic sheeting for lining the basket

Soil-less potting mix

Bucket (optional)

Plants:

Fritillaria meleagris (snake's head fritillary)

Blue *Muscari armeniacum* and white *M. armeniacum* 'Argaei Album' (grape hyacinth)

Narcissus papyraceus (paperwhite narcissus)

Primula vulgaris (primrose)

Viola × *wittrockiana* (pansy)

1 Line the basket with some moss, pushing it down well so that it stays in position. Tear off small pieces of moss and push them in place to fill any gaps in the lining.

2 Cut out a circle of plastic and push it inside the basket, tucking the edge in slightly so that it won't be visible from the outside.

3 Put some potting mix in the bottom of the basket to cover the plastic lining, making sure that there is enough room for the plants.

4 Take the plants out of their plastic pots and arrange them in the basket, using the taller plants toward the back. Pack the plants in so that the basket looks as though it is bursting with flowers.

tip:

A visit to the garden center in spring will supply you with all the plants you need for this basket, but you can also plant it with bulbs in winter and grow the plants yourself. Add pansies when the bulbs are about to flower.

5 You may find it helpful to sit the basket in a bucket to hold it steady while you are planting.

6 When you are happy with the arrangement, fill around the plants with more potting mix and push down with your fingers to hold them all in place.

7 Water the basket gently using a watering can and sit back to enjoy your springtime garden!

auricula theater

An auricula theater is a charming way to display these flowering plants. Traditionally, the background would be a dark color so that the blooms really stand out, but this softer gray sets off the colors beautifully. Auriculas are hardy plants suitable for outdoors, but good drainage is vital as they don't like sitting in very wet soil.

materials

Wooden shelves

Eggshell paint and paintbrush

Newspaper

Fine gravel

Terracotta pots, 4in (10cm) in diameter

Potting mix (4 parts soil-based potting mix for young plants, 1 part grit, and 1 part sand)

Selection of pretty auriculas:

Primula auricula

1 Wipe the shelves with a damp cloth to remove any dust and then paint them using the paintbrush, covering your work surface with some newspaper to protect it. Leave the shelves to dry and apply two coats of paint, if necessary.

2 Put some gravel in the bottom of the terracotta pots. Spoon some potting mix into each pot and remove the plants from their plastic pots. Place the plants in the terracotta pots and add a little more potting mix, leaving a gap of about ½in (1cm) at the top. Water the pots and allow to drain. Fix the shelves onto the wall and arrange the auricula pots on the shelves. Keep the potting mix moist, but not sodden, and make sure that the pots don't sit in bright sunlight.

shopping baskets

Gather together a selection of your favorite flowers and create a beautiful border in some shopping baskets, even if you have no garden at all. These baskets are made from brightly colored woven plastic that will withstand all weathers and create a blaze of color wherever they are positioned in your garden.

materials

Black plastic refuse sacks
for lining the baskets

Woven plastic shopping baskets

Drainage crocks

Potting mix

Moisture-retaining granules
(optional)

Plants:

Alchemilla mollis (lady's mantle)

Carum carvi (caraway)

Coreopsis grandiflora 'Early Sunrise' (tickseed)

Cosmos bipinnatus Sonata Series 'Sonata Carmine' and 'Sonata White'

Geum 'Prinses Juliana' (avens)

Lavandula angustifolia 'Silver Mist' (English lavender)

Primula vialii (orchid primrose)

Salvia nemorosa 'Ostfriesland'

1 Cut a few holes in the bottom of a plastic refuse sack. Open it up and place it in one of the shopping baskets, rolling the top over a little so that it sits just under the rim of the basket. Put a few crocks in the bottom of the sack for drainage.

2 Shovel potting mix into the bag until it is about half full. Add a few handfuls of moisture-retaining granules at this stage, if you wish.

tip:

Water the baskets regularly, giving a good soaking every few days in warm weather rather than a little water daily. Deadhead regularly to encourage more flowers and use a general-purpose fertilizer every couple of weeks.

3 Take the plants out of their plastic pots and loosen the roots slightly with your fingers. Place the plants in the basket, arranging them until you're happy with the positioning.

4 Add more potting mix and firm the plants into place. Give the basket a good soak with water.

vibrant planted chair

Create a riot of color with this gloriously showy flower garden. Find an old chair and remove the seat, planting it up with a vivid selection of zinnias, cosmos, and other colorful flowers. Don't worry if your woodworking skills are rather basic—once the box is painted and planted up, these won't be on show.

materials

Wooden chair without a seat

Wooden batons, 4 x 1in/ 100 x 250mm (any wood is suitable but treated wood for use outdoors has a hardier finish)

Piece of hardboard

Drill and a drill bit

Wood screws and screwdriver

Paint suitable for exterior use and paintbrush

Black plastic sheeting for lining the chair

Staple gun and staples

Drainage crocks

Potting mix

Plants:

Calibrachoa Noa Series 'Tangerine' and *C.* Superbells Series 'Raspberry' (trailing petunia)

Cosmos bipinnatus Sonata Series 'Sonata Carmine'

Gazania Sunbathers Series 'Rumi'

Osteospermum (African daisy)

Zinnia 'Zahara Mix'

1 Turn the chair upside down. Measure and cut four pieces of baton to form a box under the seat and a piece of hardboard to form the box base. Ensure the batons for the front and back edges of the box are slightly shorter at both ends (i.e. by the thickness of the batons) so they'll sit neatly between the side batons. Pre-drill three equally spaced holes along the side edges of the hardboard and one hole in the middle of the front and back edges. Pre-drill two holes in both ends of the side batons.

2 Using the pre-drilled holes, screw the piece of hardboard on top of the batons that will form the sides of the box, using wood screws.

3 Again, using the pre-drilled holes as a guide, screw the front and back batons into position between the side batons to make a sturdy box. Finally, screw the piece of hardboard in place along the front and back edges.

tip:

Deadhead the plants regularly to encourage them to produce more flowers. Water regularly in warm weather and add a soluble plant fertilizer (see page 10) every two weeks to ensure a spectacular floral display.

4 Drill a few holes in the bottom of the chair and then use the screwdriver to screw the wooden box to the underside of the seat.

5 Paint the outside of the box to match the chair, applying two coats of paint if necessary. Leave to dry completely.

6 Cut a piece of plastic to fit inside the box, making a couple of holes in it for drainage. Staple in place with the staple gun.

7 Cover the holes with drainage crocks and fill the box with potting mix until it is about half full.

8 Take the plants out of their plastic pots and arrange them in the box, using the taller plants at the back and the trailing plants around the edge. Water in well.

lavender trunk

Lavender is such a wonderful plant. With its heavenly scent and pretty flowers, it is a must in any garden. Lavender is great for encouraging bees and other insects into your garden, too, which can only be a good thing. Here, five different varieties have been used to create an abundant-looking lavender garden.

materials

Metal trunk

Drainage crocks

Fine gravel

Potting mix

Plants:

Lavandula angustifolia 'Silver Mist' (English lavender)

Lavandula 'Regal Splendour'

Lavandula stoechas 'Javelin Compact Blue,' *L. stoechas* 'Sugarberry Ruffles,' and *L. stoechas* 'Victory' (French lavender)

1 Make holes in the bottom of the trunk if necessary (see page 8). Cover the holes with a few drainage crocks and sprinkle a layer of gravel, about 1in (2.5cm) deep, into the trunk. Fill the trunk about half full with potting mix, adding a little gravel to the mix to increase drainage.

2 Take the lavender plants out of their pots and tease the roots out a little with your fingers. Arrange the plants in the trunk, positioning the taller ones toward the back. Pack more potting mix around the plants to keep them firmly in place.

tip:

Lavender thrives in full sun, so choose a nice sunny spot for your trunk. Prune the lavender plants in the fall, making sure you cut back into the green growth as they may not survive if you cut back into the old woody stems.

flowery stepladder

An old wooden stepladder adds height to a display while also being a cheap and effective way of staging plants. Handmade terracotta pots and galvanized metal buckets, planted up with pretty blooms, create a cottage-garden feel and can be displayed in the most confined of spaces.

materials

Selection of terracotta and galvanized metal pots

Drainage crocks

Potting mix

Wooden stepladder

Plants:

Armeria maritima 'Splendens' (sea thrift)

Hacquetia epipactis

Nemesia 'Mirabelle' and *N.* 'Wisley Vanilla'

Pelargonium Aristo Schoko (regal pelargonium)

Pelargonium 'Pink Capricorn' (scented-leaved pelargonium)

Saxifraga × *arendsii* 'Large White' (saxifrage)

Tiarella 'Spring Symphony' (foam flower)

Verbascum 'Pink Kisses' (mullein)

Viola 'Myfawnny' (violet)

Viola × *wittrockiana* (pansy)

1 Make sure the pots are clean before you start planting. Place a few crocks in the bottom of each pot to cover the drainage hole.

2 Put a handful of potting mix in the pot, remove the plant from its plastic pot, and place in the pot. Add more potting mix beneath the plant if necessary to raise it or remove some if the plant is sitting too high. Pack in more potting mix, firming it around the plant. Plant up the other pots, watering the plants in well, and then arrange them on the stepladder. Water the plants with a soluble plant fertilizer (see page 10) every few weeks and deadhead the flowers regularly to keep the plants in bloom.

seaside garden

A blue-and-white bowl makes the perfect container for a seaside garden. You don't have to choose plants that grow by the coast (unless you live by the sea, of course). Instead, use plants with glaucous, "whitish" leaves which will conjure up the "feel" of the seaside and work well with the thrift and agapanthus.

materials

Large enamel dish

Drainage crocks

Gravel

Potting mix

Miniature shells

Pebbles

Large shells

Plants:

Agapanthus 'Charlotte' (African lily)

Armeria maritima 'Splendens' (sea thrift)

Centaurea 'Silver Feather'

Erigeron glaucus 'Sea Breeze' (beach aster)

Lotus maculatus × *berthelotii* 'Fire Vine' (garden lotus)

1 Make holes in the base of the dish if there aren't any already (see page 8). Cover the holes with a few crocks for drainage.

2 Put a few handfuls of gravel in the bottom of the dish and add some potting mix, including a little gravel to improve drainage. Half-fill the dish with more potting mix.

tip:

Sprinkle some small pebbles over the potting mix if you can't get hold of miniature shells. You are not allowed to take pebbles from a beach, but they're usually readily available from garden centers and garden supply stores.

3 Take the plants out of their plastic pots and arrange them in the dish, spacing them out as equally as you can. Fill the dish with more potting mix, firming it around the plants with your fingers.

4 Sprinkle the miniature shells all over the surface of the potting mix to cover it and arrange the pebbles and large shells around the plants. Water in the plants.

country rose garden

Bring color and fragrance to an outside space with a rose garden. Old dolly tubs, once used for doing the laundry, can be found at car-boot and yard sales. They not only look lovely, but also provide room for roots to grow. The roses will need re-potting after a few years, but will live happily in a tub for a while if fed and pruned.

materials

Dolly tub

Drainage crocks

Potting mix suitable for roses

Perlite (optional)

Plants:

Cerastium tomentosum (snow-in-summer)

Rosa 'Chapeau de Napoléon,' *R.* 'Cornelia,' and *R.* 'Gertrude Jeykyll' (rose)

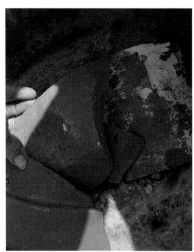

1 Make sure that the dolly tub has a few holes in the base (see page 8). Put crocks in the base of the tub, using quite a few to help with drainage.

2 Fill the tub two-thirds full with potting mix. Also add a few scoops of perlite, if you have any, at this stage to lighten the potting mix.

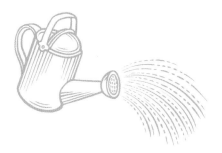

tip:

In spring mulch around the plants with well-rotted manure or garden compost. Apply rose fertilizer at the start of the growing season and again in early summer. Deadhead the roses throughout the growing season.

3 Take the roses out of their plastic pots, wearing a pair of protective gloves to guard against the thorns, and position them in the tub with the taller roses at the back. Try to disturb the roots as little as you can. Pack in some more potting mix and press down firmly.

4 Take the snow-in-summer plants out of their pots and plant them around the base of the roses. Fill any gaps with more potting mix and give the tub a thorough water.

pretty vintage tin

I like the idea of a garden that you can move round with you as you go about your day. This lovely old cookie tin has been put to good use and is now home to some pretty, small-scale plants that create a sweet little garden with a real feel of a wildflower meadow in summer.

materials

Old tin

Fine gravel

Potting mix

Plants:

Campanula pulla 'Alba' (bellflower)

Erigeron karvinskianus (fleabane)

Penstemon pinifolius 'Mersea Yellow'

Rhodanthemum catananche 'Tizi-n-Tichka'

Rhodohypoxis 'Midori'

Thymus serpyllum 'Vey'

1 Make holes in the bottom of the tin (see page 8) and cover the bottom with a layer of gravel to improve drainage. Put some potting mix on top of the layer of gravel.

2 Take the plants out of their plastic pots and gently remove some of the potting mix from around the roots. Arrange the plants in the tin, putting the taller plants toward the back. Press more potting mix around the plants and push the mix down firmly. Keep the tin well watered and remember to place it on a tray to catch the drips while you water.

metal dish displays

I love to cram lots of different plants into containers in order to create a blaze of color or a lush jungle of foliage, but sometimes less really is more. Using just three plants in some lovely old metal dishes creates a truly elegant miniature garden that has a beautiful simplicity about it.

materials

Shallow metal dishes

Long nail and hammer

Small drainage crocks

Fine gravel

Potting mix with a few handfuls of sand added

Crushed shells

Plants:

Aethionema 'Warley Rose' (stone cress)

Pink *Armeria maritima* 'Splendens' and white *A. maritima* 'Alba' (sea thrift)

Dodecatheon meadia f. *album* (shooting stars)

Jeffersonia dubia (Asian twin leaf)

Oxalis adenophylla (sauer klee)

Saxifraga 'Red Pixie' (saxifrage)

Sedum spathulifolium (stonecrop)

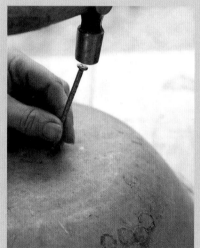

1 Make some drainage holes in the bottom of each of the metal dishes using the long nail and hammer (see page 8).

2 Cover the holes with a few small crocks for drainage and then place some of the fine gravel in the bottom of the dish.

3 Scoop potting mix into the dish. Take the plants out of their plastic pots and arrange them on top of the potting mix. Pack more mix around the plants, firming in well to hold the plants in place.

4 Cover the potting mix with some handfuls of fine gravel or crushed shells, which not only adds a decorative touch but also helps to conserve moisture. Water the plants.

tip:

Deadhead the thrift regularly and it will keep flowering. Look round garden centers for interesting materials with which to mulch the potting mix. Crushed glass, shells, and pebbles in different colors all work beautifully.

blooming buckets

Brighten up a dull corner with a group of plants that have flowers of a similar hue. Choose plants of different sizes, using big, blousy hydrangea flowers with dainty phlox, pretty verbascum, and tiarella to make a delightful floral display. Arranging some of the buckets on a bench gives the display even more impact.

materials

Collection of enamel buckets

Drainage crocks

Gravel

Potting mix

Plants:

Hydrangea macrophylla (common hydrangea)

Pelargonium Aristo Lavender (regal pelargonium)

Pelargonium 'Pink Capricorn' (scented-leaved pelargonium)

Phlox subulata 'Candy Stripes' (moss phlox)

Tiarella 'Spring Symphony' (foam flower)

Verbascum 'Pink Kisses' (mullein)

1 Put holes in the bottom of each bucket if there aren't any already (see page 8). Cover the holes with a few crocks and scoop some gravel into the bottom of the buckets to improve drainage.

2 Using a garden trowl or scoop, fill each bucket with potting mix until it is about two-thirds full.

tip:

Feed the plants with a liquid fertilizer every couple of weeks (see page 10) in order to keep them flowering well. Deadhead regularly to encourage the plants to continue flowering so you get the most from your display.

3 Take the hydrangea plant out of its plastic pot and loosen the roots a little. Put it in the first bucket so that the top of the potting mix is about 1¼in (3cm) from the rim. Add or remove potting mix beneath the plant to raise or lower it as necessary. Fill the bucket up with more potting mix. Repeat the planting process for all the other plants, trying to match the plants to the size and style of each bucket. Water all the plants in well.

wire cake stand

A simple wire cake stand can be transformed into a pretty centerpiece using dainty flowers and luscious green moss. If you are making this garden for a special occasion, plant it up about a week before you need it and keep well watered so it will be looking its best on the day.

materials

Moss (available from florists)

Three-tiered wire cake stand

Black plastic sheeting for lining the stand tiers

Potting mix

Plants:

Convallaria majalis (lily-of-the-valley)

Hedera helix (ivy)

Helianthemum 'The Bride' (rock rose)

Saxifraga 'Esther' (saxifrage)

Black *Viola* 'Molly Sanderson' and white *V.* 'Moonlight' (violet)

1 Tear off pieces of moss and push them around the edge of each tier of the cake stand.

2 For each tier, cut out a circle of plastic and make a few drainage holes with a pair of scissors. Cut a slit half way across each of the plastic circles so that they will fit over the top of the stand, and then slip them into place to form a lining.

3 Carefully scoop potting mix into each tier of the stand and press it down slightly with your fingers.

4 Take the plants out of their plastic pots and shake off any excess potting mix. Plant them in the potting mix, spreading the roots out slightly and firming around them to keep them in place.

5 Cover the surface of the potting mix with more pieces of moss, tucking them around the rim of each tier. Water each tier thoroughly.

tip:

If your local garden center does not sell any moss for lining the stand, then try a florist shop because they will usually stock some. Make sure that the moss is kept damp so that it will keep its fresh green color.

suitcase garden

Regard any container as a potential garden. This old-fashioned suitcase is ideal for creating a miniature garden. I love hellebores and the fact that they appear after a gloomy winter only adds to their appeal. The muted colors of these pulsatillas and hellebores look beautiful, but brightly colored plants would look fabulous, too.

materials

Black plastic refuse sack for lining the suitcase

Old suitcase

Drainage crocks

Potting mix with a few handfuls of sand added

Plants:

Helleborus argutifolius (Corsican hellebore)

Helleborus lividus (hellebore)

Pulsatilla vulgaris and *P. vulgaris* 'Eva Constance' (pasque flower)

1 Cut a plastic refuse sack down so that it will fit snugly inside the suitcase and form a lining. Push the sack neatly into the corners. Use a pair of scissors to cut some holes in the plastic for drainage. If you want to keep the suitcase in good condition, simply leave the lining intact and make sure you do not overwater.

2 Put some crocks in the bottom of the suitcase, covering the holes in the plastic to help improve the drainage.

3 Fill the suitcase with potting mix, stopping just short of the top of the refuse-sack lining.

4 Take the plants out of their plastic pots and position them in the suitcase until you are happy with the arrangement. Scoop out some of the potting mix and push the plants into the holes, firming around the plants to keep them in place.

tip:

Water the garden, but make sure that the roots are not sitting in too much water, especially if there are no holes in the plastic lining. This is because both hellebores and pulsatillas like moist but well-drained soil.

fabulous foliage

fern terrarium

Select an open-topped vase to create an indoor garden in a terrarium. Choose plants with similar needs, mixing colors and textures for more interest, and make sure they are not too big. You can buy a potting mix specifically designed for terrariums from garden centers or make your own (see the Materials panel).

materials

Large glass vase

Pea gravel

Ground charcoal (available from pet stores)

Slightly damp potting mix (the ideal mix for these plants is soil-less potting mix with a little added sand and some perlite or vermiculite, if desired)

Fine gravel

Water spray bottle for misting the plants

Plants:

Adiantum raddianum (Delta maidenhair fern)

Oxalis triangularis (purple shamrock)

Selaginella kraussiana (Krauss' spikemoss)

1 Wash and dry the vase to make sure it is spotlessly clean. Carefully put some pea gravel in the bottom of the vase to form a layer about 1in (2.5cm) deep. Even off the surface so that it is quite flat.

2 Spoon some ground charcoal over the top of the pea gravel to form another layer of about the same depth. This will reduce the odor caused by the damp potting mix.

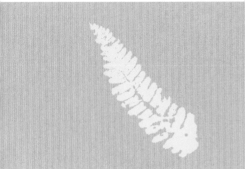

3 Sprinkle a little more potting mix on top of the charcoal to cover it completely. Take the plants out of their plastic pots and arrange them in the vase. Put handfuls of potting mix around the plants to hold them firmly in place, covering their roots. Even off the surface of the mix as much as you can.

tip:

Check the potting mix weekly and pour a little water into the terrarium if it feels dry. Check the plants don't look too wet or too dry, and alter the watering accordingly. Mist the plants occasionally with a spray bottle.

4 Wipe the inside of the glass with a clean cloth in order to remove any potting mix or charcoal. Sprinkle some fine gravel around the plants over the surface of the potting mix to a depth of about ½in (1cm) and then level off again.

5 Spray the plants with a fine misting of water using the water spray bottle.

fabulous foliage 69

green-roof birdhouse

Green roofs are very popular at the moment and are a wonderful way of encouraging wildlife onto what would otherwise be wasted space. Spot the potential in even the smallest of spaces and create a green roof on a birdhouse. Only basic woodwork skills are needed and a slightly rough finish adds to the overall charm.

materials

Exterior-grade sawn timber, 1½ x ¾in (35 x 20mm)

Wooden birdhouse

Drill and drill bit

Wood screws and screwdriver

Eco-friendly water-based paint suitable for external use and safe for birds plus a paintbrush

Black plastic sheeting for lining the roof

Staple gun and staples

Potting mix with some added grit

Selection of saxifrages and sedums:

Saxifraga 'Cloth of Gold' (saxifrage)

Sedum acre 'Golden Queen,' *S. oregonense*, *S. pluricaule*, *S. spathulifolium* 'Purpureum,' *S. spurium* 'Fuldaglut' (stonecrop)

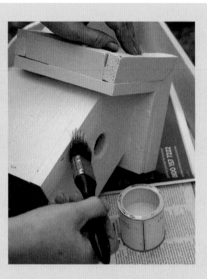

1 Measure and cut four wooden batons from the sawn timber to fit along the front and back edges of the birdhouse roof, angling one end of each of them so that they marry up at the top. Pre-drill holes in the wood and screw the wooden batons onto the roof. Measure and cut another two batons to fit along the side edges of the roof, pre-drilling and screwing them between the front and back pieces, as shown.

2 Paint the whole birdhouse and then leave it to dry thoroughly. Apply two layers of paint if necessary.

3 Cut a piece of plastic to line the roof and staple it inside the roof using the staple gun. Fold the plastic at the corners to achieve a snug fit.

4 Press some potting mix onto the lining. Take the plants out of their pots and break them up into smaller pieces. Spread out the roots to flatten them slightly and then push the plants into the mix, pressing the mix down firmly. Continue planting until the roof is covered. Keep in a sheltered spot for a couple of weeks so that the roots can mesh together and form a solid mat which will hold the plants in place.

tip:

Once the roots of the little plants have meshed together, the green roof will be fairly robust and require little maintenance. You'll need to water the roof in particularly dry weather but otherwise just sit back and enjoy!

desert garden glasses

This tiny cacti and succulent garden brings a touch of the desert to your table. The ground shells make a pretty top dressing and also have a lovely texture, although sand would work just as well. Placing the glass tumblers in a decorative holder means that you can move your little garden around without injury.

materials

Small glass tumblers in a holder

Ground shells

Small kitchen tongs

Plants:

Aloe claviflora

Echeveria setosa var. *deminuta* (Mexican firecracker)

Euphorbia enopla (spurge)

Euphorbia horrida var. *striata* (spurge)

Oreocereus trollii

Pachyphytum oviferum (moonstone)

1 Clean the glass tumblers and dry them thoroughly. Spoon some of the ground shells into the bottom of each glass. Using the kitchen tongs, put one plant (still in its plastic pot) in each tumbler, adding more ground shells underneath if necessary so that the rim of the pot is about ¾in (2cm) lower than the rim of the tumbler.

2 Sprinkle more of the shells into the tumblers, completely covering the pots and the surface of the potting mix. Tap the side of each tumbler gently to level off the shell mixture. The tumblers don't have drainage holes, so you'll have to water the plants carefully as overwatering may cause the plants to rot. Water about once every two weeks in summer and less over the winter. Check the moisture level of the potting mix, using a small stick, and then water accordingly.

fairy garden

Create a miniature oasis to welcome fairies into your garden. An elegant stone urn is ideal, but any pot or dish with a wide rim will do. I have chosen plants with small-scale foliage and flowers, adding toadstools, little pine cones in a basket, and some tiny gardening tools to help the fairies keep the garden looking good.

materials

Stone urn

Drainage crocks

Soil-less potting mix

Hand pruners (secateurs)

Twigs

Waterproof adhesive

Moss available from florists

Flat pebbles for the path

Fairy accessories such as miniature toadstools

Clothes pin and raffia for the fairy (optional)

Plants:

Allium cyaneum (dark blue garlic)

Anemone blanda (windflower)

Leucojum aestivum (summer snowflake)

Primula vulgaris (common primrose) for fairy hat and skirt

Saxifraga × apiculata 'Alba' (saxifrage)

Trifolium repens 'Purpurascens' (ornamental clover)

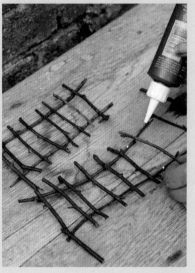

1 Clean out the urn. Cover the drainage hole in the base with a few crocks and then fill with potting mix, stopping about 1in (2.5cm) from the rim.

2 To make a fence, use the hand pruners to cut two lengths of twig about 7in (18cm) long; two lengths about 4in (10cm) long; and 7 lengths about 3in (8cm) long. Lay the longest pieces horizontally on a table, about 2½in (6cm) apart, and glue the two middle-length pieces across both ends. Glue the short lengths onto the top and bottom, and leave to dry completely before moving. Repeat to make two fences.

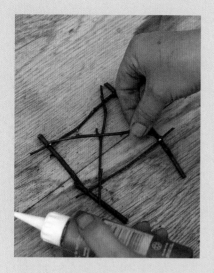

3 To make the gate, measure and cut two lengths of twig 4in (10cm) long, and lay them vertically on the table, about 3in (8cm) apart. Cut two thinner twigs 4in (10cm) long and glue them onto the top and bottom of the first twigs to form a square. Measure and cut two thin twigs 4½in (11cm) long and glue them to form a cross shape on the gate. Again, leave to dry thoroughly before moving.

4 Take the plants out of their plastic pots and position them on the potting mix to make a pleasing arrangement. Scoop out a little of the potting mix and place a plant in the hole, backfilling around it and pressing down the potting mix firmly. Tear off a sheet of moss to cover the bare potting mix, tucking it neatly around the plants. Push the fences and the gate into the moss, adjusting the gate so that it is slightly open.

5 Place pebbles on the moss to make a path for the fairies and add miniature toadstools (either store-bought or made from some modeling clay) and other fairy accessories to finish off.

tip:

If the fairies in your area are a little shy, you can easily make your own with a wooden clothes pin. Create a fairy dress with primula leaves, tied to the body with a raffia bow, and add a flower hat to finish.

succulents in drawers

Old wooden drawers of varying shapes and sizes make great containers for a succulent garden. Succulents have shallow root systems so do not need particularly deep containers. These drawers had gaps in the joints, so I didn't need to make drainage holes, but you can drill a few holes in each drawer before you start.

materials

Selection of wooden drawers in different sizes

Gravel

Potting mix with a few handfuls of sand added

Fine gravel

Selection of succulents such as:

Aeonium 'Zwartkop'

Crassula ovata (money plant)

Crassula rupestris var. *marnieriana* (jade necklace)

Echeveria gibbiflora var. *metallica*

Echeveria secunda var. *glauca*

Graptopetalum paraguayense (ghost plant)

Jovibarba sobolifera

Saxifraga cuneifolia (shield-leaved saxifrage)

Sedum rupestre, S. rupestre 'Angelina,' and *S. rupestre* 'Aureum' (stone orpine)

1 Arrange the drawers on the surface where you will eventually display your succulent garden. Make sure that all of the drawers are stable.

2 Put a few handfuls of the coarser gravel in the bottom of each drawer to help with drainage.

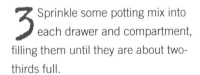

tip:

The garden should be kept in a warm, sheltered spot. Protect it from too much rain if you can and provide good drainage by putting holes in the drawers and plenty of sand in the potting mix if they are in a very exposed site.

3 Sprinkle some potting mix into each drawer and compartment, filling them until they are about two-thirds full.

4 Take the plants out of their plastic pots and remove any excess potting mix. Plant them in the drawers, spreading out the roots as much as you can. Add more potting mix to hold the plants in place.

5 Cover the surface of the potting mix with the fine gravel, which will help prevent the leaves of the plants rotting if they come into contact with the surface. Water and leave to drain.

tip:

Tear off pieces of moss and use them to hide the potting mix if you like. Keep the moss watered so that it retains its color. These conifers will need re-potting after the first year, adding fertilizer to encourage growth.

topiary garden

These miniature conifers, with their different shades of green and interesting foliage textures, make a very cute little garden. Any small containers will work, but these sweet galvanized tubs work especially well. Alternatively, you can plant the conifers in one big galvanized tub to create a miniature evergreen forest.

materials

Small galvanized buckets

Drainage crocks

Gravel

Potting mix

Moss (available from florists)

Plants:

Chamaecyparis lawsoniana 'Ellwoodii,' *C. lawsoniana* 'Ellwood's Gold,' *C. lawsoniana* 'Snow White' (Lawson cypress)

Chamaecyparis pisifera 'Boulevard' (Sawara cypress)

Thuja occidentalis 'Teddy' (white cedar)

Thuja plicata Goldy (Western red cedar)

1 Make a few holes in the bottom of the buckets (see page 8) and cover with a few drainage crocks. Put a little gravel in the bottom of each bucket.

2 Scoop a little potting mix into the first bucket. Take the plant out of its plastic pot and put it in the bucket. Make sure that the surface of the plant is an inch or so from the rim of the bucket and fill around it with more potting mix. Plant up the rest of the buckets in the same way. You may wish to cover the potting mix with some moss.

colander baskets

Hanging baskets are an ideal way to garden when you have limited space. These old colanders were planted with ferns and potato vines, and then hung up with hooks and chains which are readily available from DIY stores. Fix brackets to a wall to hang the colanders or attach hooks to a pergola, for example.

materials

Hanging basket linings

Old colanders

Potting mix

Moisture-retaining granules

6½ft (2m) of chain per colander

4 S-shaped hooks per colander

1 keyring hoop per colander

Hooks or nails for suspending the colanders

Plants:

Cyrtomium fortunei var. *clivicola* (Japanese holly fern)

Dryopteris atrata (shaggy shield fern)

Ipomoea batatus 'Sweet Caroline Bronze' (sweet potato vine)

Polystichum makinoi (Makinoi's holly fern)

1 Put a hanging basket lining inside the colander, trimming it down if necessary so that it sits snugly inside.

2 Put a little potting mix in the bottom of the colander and add a handful of moisture-retaining granules. Remove the plant from its plastic pot and place in the colander.

3 Fill around the plant with potting mix, firming it in well so that it is held in place. Water thoroughly.

4 Measure and cut four lengths of chain, each 20in (50cm) long. Attach an S-shaped hook onto one end of each chain and close the hooks slightly using a pair of pliers.

5 Thread the other end of each chain onto a keyring hoop, ready to suspend your colander garden in its chosen location.

6 Thread the S-shaped hooks though holes in the colander, positioning them evenly around the colander so that it will hang level.

7 Plant the other colanders in the same way and suspend them by hanging the hoops from hooks or nails.

tip:

Water the colanders regularly, making sure they don't dry out, and feed about once a month (see page 10). Keep the shade-loving ferns out of direct sunlight and shelter both these and the potato vines from frost.

dinosaur swamp garden

Create a den for your children's favorite model dinosaurs and encourage hours of creative play. Choose plants that are fairly robust and able to withstand dinosaur stampedes! Also make sure that they are relatively easy to look after so your children can enjoy cultivating their garden, as well as playing with it.

materials

Enamel dish

Drainage crocks

Pea gravel

Potting mix

Piece of thick black plastic for the pond

Pebbles and stones

Plants:

Blechnum spicant (hard fern)

Crassula muscosa (watch-chain plant)

Crassula ovata (money plant)

Haworthia attenuata (zebra plant)

Lampranthus 'Apricot'

Sagina subulata var. *glabrata* (golden pearlwort)

Soleirolia soleirolii (mind-your-own-business)

1 Make holes in the bottom of the enamel dish for drainage (see page 8) if there aren't any already. Cover the holes with some drainage crocks and place a layer of pea gravel in the bottom. Scoop some potting mix into the dish.

2 Take the plants out of their plastic pots and plant them around the edge of the enamel dish, firming in the potting mix with your fingers to hold them in place.

3 Cut a circle of black plastic, about 10in (25cm) in diameter. Form a dip in the potting mix and push the circle of plastic into it to make the pond liner. Arrange pebbles and stones around the edge of the plastic to anchor it down.

4 Fill in the gaps with pieces of mind-your-own-business and golden pearlwort to complete the garden planting.

5 Fill the pond with a little water and then introduce your dinosaurs to their exciting new home!

tiny terrariums

These terrariums use tumbers as their containers. Look for small plants with shallow roots that will live happily in little containers. Tiny succulents are ideal and look striking with sand and shells. Provide the terrariums with some direct sunlight, as succulents like lots of light, and also ventilation—a windowsill is ideal.

materials

Glass tumblers

Specialty potting mix suitable for cacti and succulents

Fine gravel and sand

Kitchen tongs

Miniature shells

Plants:

Back tumbler: *Adromischus leucophyllus* and *Aeonium* 'Zwartkop'

Second tumbler from back: *Pachyphytum oviferum* (moonstone)

Third tumbler from back: *Lapidaria margaretae* (Karoo rose), *Sempervivum* (houseleek)

Front tumbler: *Anacampseros telephiastrum* 'Variegata,' *Crassula rupestris* var. *marnieriana* (jade necklace), and *Echeveria setosa* var. *deminata* (Mexican firecracker)

1 Clean the glass tumblers and make sure they are free of dust and grease. Spoon a little potting mix into the bottom of each tumbler.

2 For each glass tumbler, make a small dip in the potting mix. Remove the plant(s) from their plastic pots and push them into the tumbler, firming in the mix slightly with the end of a spoon. Repeat with the remaining plants and tumblers.

tip:

The plants in the tumblers are all different varieties of succulent that prefer very dry conditions, so make sure you don't overwater the terrariums as this may cause the plants to rot. The mix should be moist, but not too wet.

3 Carefully spoon gravel or sand into each glass, completely covering the potting mix and trying not to get too much on the plants.

4 Tap each tumbler gently against the palm of your hand in order to settle the gravel or sand. Using the small tongs, add decorative touches such as miniature shells to the tumblers, arranging them carefully.

vertical garden

Vertical gardens are popular at the moment and perfect for small spaces. This garden is made from a wooden box filled with succulents that are relatively maintenance-free and look beautiful, too. I found a box with dividers, but you can staple the wire mesh around the edge of the box if it does not have these.

materials

Wooden drinks box

Potting mix with a few handfuls of perlite or vermiculite added

Wire mesh

Wire cutters or strong scissors

Staple gun and staples

Moss (available from florists)

Plants:

Top row: *Sempervivum* 'Rosie' (houseleek), *Saxifraga cuneifolia* (shield-leaved saxifrage), *Echeveria gibbiflora* var. metallica, *Crassula rupestris* var. marnieriana (jade necklace), *Sempervivum* 'Lilac Time'

Middle row: *Delosperma cooperi*, *Sedum acre* 'Golden Queen,' (stonecrop), *Saxifraga* 'Tumbling Waters,' *Sempervivum* 'Blood Tip,' *Sedum spathulifolium*

Bottom row: *Sedum pluricaule*, *Sempervivum ruthenicum*, *Sedum spathulifolium* 'Purpureum,' *Saxifraga* 'Pearly King,' *Sempervivum* 'Dark Cloud'

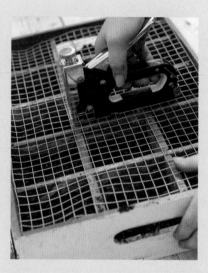

1 Fill the wooden box two-thirds full with potting mix, pressing it down with your fingers in order to compact it.

2 Measure and cut a piece of wire mesh with the wire cutters or scissors (wearing protective gloves if necessary) so that it fits snugly inside the box. If you are attaching the wire to the outside of the box, then simply cut it a little bigger. Staple the wire mesh into place, making sure it is secure.

3 Using the wire cutters or scissors, cut a vertical hole in the mesh and then make a small line of cuts at the top and bottom of the first one in order to create two flaps that you can open out a little.

4 Take a plant out of its plastic pot, remove any excess potting mix, and carefully push the roots though the hole. Pack in as much potting mix as possible and then bend the flaps over as far as you can without damaging the plant.

5 Continue to plant up the box, making sure that each plant contrasts with its neighbor. Check that all the plants are held firmly in place. Water in well.

tip:

Lay the box flat and water it about once a week in summer and once a month in winter. Let the potting mix dry out between waterings. Succulents don't like sitting in very wet soil, so be sure not to over water.

6 Keep the box flat for about two weeks to give the roots a chance to grow and settle into the box a little. Add a few pieces of moss to fill in any gaps if you wish to cover the wire mesh. After that time, the box can be hung vertically, following the watering guide described in the "Tip" on the left. It is best to keep your vertical garden in a sheltered spot over the winter.

tip:

The water in the bowl will look cloudy and murky initially, but it will become clear as the plants settle down. Scoop out brown leaves or broken roots, if there are any, in order to keep the water garden nice and clear.

lush water garden

Make a miniature water garden using a plain, deep-sided bowl, and add some pebbles and water plants in order to create a lush tabletop pond. Using old cups and bottles to hold the plants adds an interesting decorative touch and also disguises some of the thicker plant roots.

materials

Large glass bowl

Pebbles

Old enamel cup

Vintage stone bottles or similar

Plants:

Caltha natans (floating marsh marigold)

Hippuris vulgaris (mare's tail)

Ludwigia palustris (water purslane)

Pistia stratiotes (water lettuce)

Salvinia natans (water velvet)

1 Clean the bowl thoroughly and make sure that it is free of grease. Arrange the pebbles in the bottom of the bowl. Use a jug to pour water into the bowl, filling it about three-quarters full.

2 Use the old cup and bottles to hold the deep-rooted plants in place. Immerse the cup and bottles in the water and carefully push the roots of a plant inside, using the small bottles for the smallest plants. Push the cup and bottles down to the bottom of the bowl, moving the pebbles so that they sit directly on the bottom of the bowl. Lay the floating plants on top of the water.

exotic bog garden

These wonderful plants look as if they're from another planet. Strikingly beautiful, they have the added bonus of being relatively trouble-free. They need to be in wet soil at all times and should be watered with rainwater because tap water may be too alkaline. If you can't get hold of rainwater, then use distilled water instead.

materials

Gravel

Galvanized metal basket with a solid base

Potting mix with a little sand added

Plants:

Dionaea muscipula
(Venus fly trap)

Sarracenia 'Cowboy'
(pitcher plant)

Sarracenia leucophylla
(white trumpet)

Sarracenia × *wrigleyana*
(pitcher plant)

1 Using a garden trowel or scoop, put a thin layer of gravel in the bottom of the basket.

2 Fill the basket with potting mix until it is about two-thirds full. Remember to incorporate some sand into the potting mix as you go.

tip:

The bog garden must be very moist to keep the plants happy. The plants can feed themselves, so no extra plant food is needed. Pitcher plants are fairly hardy and can withand frosts, but require a sheltered spot in the winter.

3 Take the plants out of their plastic pots and arrange them in the basket, placing the taller ones in the center and the shorter ones around the edge.

4 Add some more potting mix around each of the plants and firm them in using your fingers. Water in the plants.

cake-stand terrarium

A pretty glass cake stand with a translucent cloche lid makes a fun and effective container for a terrarium. Choose two or three plants that like humid conditions and then plant them up with some moss. You can also add a few well-chosen pebbles to decorate the scene if you wish.

materials

Fine gravel

Glass cake stand with domed lid

Ground charcoal (available from pet stores)

Potting mix

Moss (available from florists)

Pebbles

Water spray bottle for misting the plants

Plants:

Humata tyermanii (bunny fern)

Peperomia obtusifolia 'Variegata' (baby rubber plant)

Tradescantia zebrina (wandering Jew)

1 Spread some fine gravel over the base of the cake stand. Make sure that you keep the gravel away from the edge of the stand so that the lid will fit on.

2 Spread a few scoops of ground charcoal over the layer of gravel, to help keep odors down.

3 Shovel potting mix onto the stand, forming it into a slightly domed shape.

4 Lay the moss over the potting mix and trim around the edge with some scissors, putting the lid on to make sure it fits.

5 Tear holes in the moss and push the plants through, firming the moss around them to keep them in place.

tip:

Keep the cake-stand terrarium out of direct sunlight, but somewhere warm. Remove the cloche lid from time to time in order to air the plants. Remember to keep the potting mix and moss moist, but not too wet.

6 Arrange the pebbles on the moss. Water sparingly and mist the plants slightly with the water spray bottle. Put the lid back on.

crops
in pots

herb trolley

A herb trolley is a great way to grow lots of herbs when space is limited. This trolley was bought new, but look for old ones at yard sales. A plastic vegetable rack would work well, too. It may seem obvious, but only grow herbs that you enjoy and cook with. There is no point nurturing herbs you are unlikely to use or eat.

materials

Black plastic refuse sacks
for lining the tiers of the trolley

Tiered metal trolley

Fine gravel

Small pebbles

Potting mix

Selection of herbs such as:

Foeniculum vulgare (fennel)

Galium odoratum
(sweet woodruff)

Origanum majorana
(sweet marjoram)

Origanum vulgare (oregano)

Petroselinum crispum (parsley)

Salvia officinalis (common sage)

Thymus vulgaris (thyme)

1 Cut a piece of refuse sack to fit in each shelf of the trolley. Make a few slits in the plastic so that water will be able to drain through.

2 Add an inch or so of the fine gravel on top of the plastic lining and spread it out evenly. Put a few small pebbles on top of the gravel to provide extra drainage.

3 Put potting mix into each shelf of the trolley, filling the shelves until they are about half full.

4 Take the plants out of their plastic pots and shake off any excess potting mix. Scoop out a little potting mix from the first shelf and put in the plants, adding some more mix to hold them in place. Continue planting all the shelves of the trolley, filling the top shelf with plants and placing plants around the edges of the shelves underneath. Water well.

tip:

Water the trolley regularly, and you will have a supply of herbs through the growing season. Feed the herbs with plant fertilizer (see page 10) every couple of weeks during the growing season, and cut and eat them regularly.

salad in a tub

This is the perfect garden to have by your back door. Being able to pick fresh salad daily is one of the highlights of summer and you really don't need much space at all. I bought these plants for the tub, but you can grow the leaves from seed first (which is even more economical), although they will take longer to crop.

materials

Galvanized metal tub

Drainage crocks

Pea gravel

Potting mix

Bendy twigs (optional)

Plants:

Eruca vesicaria subsp. *sativa* (arugula/salad rocket)

Latuca sativa (cut-and-come-again lettuce)

Rumex acetosa (I used common and broad-leaved sorrel)

Rumex sanguineus (red-veined sorrel)

Viola × *wittrockiana* (pansy)

1 Make holes in the bottom of the tub if you need to (see page 8). Place a few crocks over the holes to help with drainage.

2 Add a layer of pea gravel to the bottom of the tub before filling with some potting mix until it nearly reaches the rim.

3 Making a little twiggy fence to sit around the perimeter of the tub is, of course, optional but gives the tub the look of a traditional kitchen garden. To make the fence, simply cut lengths of twig about 16in (40cm) long. Bend one into an arch and push it firmly into the potting mix. Continue with the other twig arches, overlapping them to make a neat edging to the tub.

4 Scoop out a little of the potting mix and push in the plants, firming around each one as you go to keep them in place.

5 Space the plants an inch (2.5cm) or so apart (although I usually cram as many plants as possible into a pot because the leaves tend to taste better when picked small and you are also more likely to harvest them regularly in small quantities). Keep the potting mix moist, watering throughout the growing season, and pick the leaves regularly to prevent the plants running to seed.

tip:

Edible flowers add pretty splashes of color to the tub, as well as having a practical use. Grow nasturtium, calendula, and zucchini (courgette) flowers to use in salads. These also attract aphid-eating insects such as ladybirds.

guttering gardens

This garden is based on a method used by gardeners to start off pea crops by planting the seeds in guttering before transferring the seedlings to a bigger container. The peas can be eaten as pea shoots, cutting off the tips to eat before they develop into pods. Colorful flowers and foliage make the garden even more attractive.

materials

Hacksaw or similar

Lengths of guttering with end pieces

Medium-grade sandpaper

Fixings for the guttering (brackets and screws)

Paint suitable for exterior use and paintbrush

Drill and drill bit

Gravel

Potting mix

Plants:

Calibrachoa Noa Series 'Tangerine' and *C.* Superbells Series 'Raspberry' (trailing petunia)

Eruca vesicaria subsp. *sativa* (arugula/salad rocket)

Lactuca sativa (red-leaved lettuce)

Lactuca sativa var. *longifolia* (romaine/cos lettuce)

Lamium maculatum 'Aureum' (dead nettle)

Pisum sativum (peas)

1 Using the hacksaw, cut two lengths of guttering, about 30in (75cm) in length. Rub sandpaper all over the guttering, end pieces, and brackets to make the surfaces rough so that the paint will adhere well.

2 Using the paintbrush, paint the guttering, end pieces, and brackets, leaving the inside of the guttering unpainted. Apply two coats of paint if necessary and leave to dry.

3 Decide where you want to display your garden, mark the position for the brackets, and then screw them into the wall.

4 Slide the lengths of guttering onto the brackets, pushing them firmly into place. Re-touch any scratches with some more paint. Fix the end pieces into position, clipping them on securely. Drill a few holes in the bottom of the pieces of guttering for drainage.

5 Sprinkle a little gravel along the lengths of guttering and then cover this with a layer of potting mix.

tip:

It's lovely to have lots of crops to harvest in the summer, so include arugula (rocket) and small lettuce plants. These can be picked regularly to keep the plants small and provide you with a constant supply of salad leaves.

6 Take the plants out of their trays or plastic pots and plant them in the guttering. Water in well.

berries in a bread bin

A bread bin is an ideal container for a gooseberry bush as there is lots of room for the roots to grow. Make more of the space by planting a few strawberry plants with pretty flowers and delicious fruits around the base of the gooseberry. Birds will love your fruit garden, too, so add a fabric bird scarer to help protect the berries.

materials

Old enamel bread bin

Drainage crocks

Gravel

Potting mix

A couple of twiggy sticks

String

Strips of pretty fabric

Plants:

Fragaria × *ananassa* (strawberry)

Ribes uva-crispum (gooseberry)

1 Make holes in the bottom of the bread bin if you need to (see page 8). Cover these holes with a few drainage crocks.

2 Add a few handfuls of gravel to the bottom of the bread bin. Fill the bin until it is about two-thirds full with potting mix.

3 Take the gooseberry bush out of its plastic pot—carefully and using protective gloves! Loosen the roots and put it into the bin toward the back. Pack more potting mix around the plant, making sure that it is not planted too deeply as this can encourage suckers to grow.

tip:
You will need to feed the gooseberry bush with a sprinkling of sulphate of potash, either in winter or early spring. Early spring is also a good time of year to mulch the plants in the bin with garden compost or manure.

4 Take the strawberry plants out of their pots and arrange them around the front of the bin, adding more potting mix around them and firming it in to hold the plants in place. Water the tub.

5 To make a bird scarer, push a stick into either side of the bin and tie a piece of string to both sticks. Tear strips of fabric, about 12in (30cm) long, and tie them onto the string to frighten away the birds.

kids' edible garden

As well as looking beautiful, this little garden is also appealing to little fingers as the plants are all easy to grow and most can be eaten. Children may wish to grow the plants from seed themselves and then plant up the trug when the plants are big enough or you can just buy small plugs from the garden center.

materials

Metal trug

Drainage crocks

Gravel

Potting mix

Moisture-retaining granules (optional)

Plants:

Calendula officinalis (pot marigold)

Fragaria × ananassa 'Sarian F1' and 'Merlan F1' (strawberry)

Helianthus annus (sunflower)

Lactuca sativa (red-leaved lettuce)

Lactuca sativa var. *longifolia* (romaine/cos lettuce)

Lycopersicon esculentum 'Lidi' (cherry tomato)

Ocimum basilicum var. *purpurascens* (purple basil)

Petroselinum crispum (parsley)

Raphanus sativus 'Cherry Belle' (radish)

1 Make holes in the base of the trug if necessary (see page 8). Cover the holes with drainage crocks and put a layer of gravel in the bottom of the trug.

2 Put some potting mix in the trug, adding a couple of handfuls of moisture-retaining granules if you have any, which will help prevent the trug drying out.

3 Remove the sunflower from its plastic pot and plant it at the back of the trug.

4 Arrange all the other plants around the sunflower, cramming in as many as you can. Water the basket in well.

tip:

Feed the plants with a tomato fertilizer to encourage the production of lots of fruits on the strawberry and tomato plants. Your children can help you make sure the trug does not dry out by watering it regularly.

herb buckets

Fresh herbs are easy to grow and are fabulous to have in the kitchen, too. Choose a spot near your back door where you can fasten some decorative hooks and then plant up some buckets with a selection of herbs such as oregano, thyme, and mint. Keep scissors nearby so you can cut the herbs as you need them.

materials

Selection of galvanized buckets or lanterns (any metal containers with a handle will do)

Moss (optional)

Drainage crocks

Potting mix

Hooks and screws

Selection of herbs such as:

Mentha suaveolens 'Variegata' (pineapple mint)

Origanum vulgare 'Aureum' (golden marjoram)

Thymus vulgaris (thyme)

1 Make holes in the bottom of the buckets and lanterns if they do not already have them (see page 8). If you are using a lantern, push some pieces of moss inside to stop the potting mix from falling out.

2 Place a few crocks in the bottom of each bucket or lantern to cover over the drainage holes.

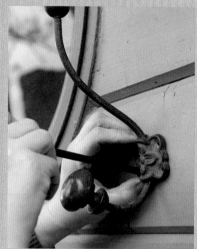

3 Put a few scoops of potting mix inside the bucket or lantern. Take the plant from its plastic pot and loosen the roots slightly. Place inside the lantern and fill with more potting mix. Plant up the remaining buckets or lanterns and buckets with herbs in the same way. Water all the containers thoroughly.

4 Screw some hooks into the wall and hang the buckets and lanterns from them. Check the potting mix regularly to ensure that it is moist.

5 If you hang the buckets and lanterns close to your kitchen door, you'll easily be able to snip fresh herbs when cooking.

tip:

It is important not to let the herbs dry out, as they will quickly wilt. If they do become very dry, immerse the buckets and lanterns in water for 15 minutes to soak them through and then re-hang them on their hooks.

vegetable crate

You may not have thought it possible to grow vegetables without a garden. Whet your appetite for vegetable growing by using a wooden crate that will be as lovely to look at as it is practical. You won't produce enough for the whole summer, but you'll get a few pickings and be able to enjoy growing your own food from seed.

materials

Black plastic refuse sack

Wooden crate

Drainage crocks

Potting mix

Sharp (horticultural) sand

Short stick or garden cane

Plant labels

Twigs for staking beans and peas

Seeds of the following crops:

Beta vulgaris (beets/beetroot)

Daucus carota (carrot)

Phaseolus vulgaris (green/French bean)

Pisum sativum (pea)

1 Cut a few slits in the bottom of the refuse sack and open it up. Roll down the top and push it into the crate. You can staple the bag onto the crate if you like to keep it in place but this is optional, as the potting mix should keep it in place. Place a few drainage crocks over the holes in the bag. Fill the plastic liner with potting mix, adding a few handfuls of sand and mixing it in to the area where the carrots are to grow.

2 Lay the short stick or garden cane on the surface of the potting mix across the crate to use as a guide for sowing the seeds. Pour some seeds into the palm of your hand and sprinkle a few sparingly along the side of the stick or cane.

4 Write a plant label and push it into the potting mix at one end of the line of seeds. Cover the seeds with a little more potting mix. Repeat this for all of the seeds, sowing two lines of carrots, two lines of beets (beetroot), two lines of peas, and one line of green (French) beans. Sow the seed for the peas and beans about 10cm (4in) apart and 1¼in (3cm) deep. Make sure that all of the lines of seed are clearly labeled.

5 Water the seeds in, making sure you use a fine rose attachment on the watering can so that you don't disturb the seeds.

6 Thin out the carrot and beet seedlings as they grow so that eventually the plants are spaced about 2in (5cm) apart.

tip:
Keep the potting mix in the crate moist. Check the crate in the evenings to catch any visiting slugs and snails. Also, stake the peas and beans as they get taller by tying them to sticks pushed into the potting mix.

resources

United Kingdom

Alexandra Nurseries
Estate House
Parish Lane
Penge
London SE20 7LJ
020 8778 4145
www.alexandranurseries.co.uk

Lovely selection of plants, plus vintage garden and homeware

Anthropologie
00800 0026 8476 (international freephone)
www.anthropologie.eu
Ornate garden accessories and homeware

Crocus
0844 557 2244
www.crocus.co.uk

Great mail-order nursery selling a wide selection of plants and accessories

Drointon Nurseries
Plaster Pitts
Norton Conyers
Ripon
North Yorkshire HG4 5EF
01765 641849
www.auricula-plants.co.uk

Specialist primula auricula nursery, offering a wide selection of auriculas and advice on planting

Lilies Water Gardens
Broad Lane
Newdigate
Surrey RH5 5AT
01306 631064
www.lilieswatergardens.co.uk

Nursery specializing in water plants

Mabel and Rose
01993 778885
www.mabelandrose.com

Lovely selection of vintage garden accessories available through an on-line shop

Petersham Nurseries
Church Lane (off Petersham Road)
Richmond
Surrey TW10 7AG
020 8940 5230
www.petershamnurseries.co.uk

Beautiful selection of plants and vintage containers

RE
Bishops Yard
Main Street
Corbridge
Northumberland NE45 5LA
01434 634567
www.re-foundobjects.com

Lovely baskets and vintage finds available mail-order

RHS Wisley Garden
Woking
GU23 6QB
0845 260 9000
www.rhs.org.uk/gardens/wisley

Inspirational gardens and a fantastic plant center with a wide selection of alpines, plus an advice center for RHS members

Sarah Raven's Kitchen Garden
0845 092 0283
www.sarahraven.com

Beautiful selection of seeds, plants, and bulbs by post

The Secret Garden Centre
Coxwell Road
70 Westow Street
Upper Norwood
London SE19 3AF
020 8771 8200
www.thesecretgardencentre.com

Small garden center with a good selection of plants and accessories

Slack Top Nurseries
1 Waterloo House
Slack Top
Hebden Bridge HX7 7HA
01422 845348
www.slacktopnurseries.co.uk

Specialist alpine nursery offering mail-order service

United States and Canada

Anthropologie (across USA)
(800) 309-2500
www.anthropologie.com
Ornate garden accessories and homeware

Ben Wolff
279 Sharon Turnpike
Goshen
Connecticut 06756
(860) 618-2317
www.benwolffpottery.com

Traditional and modern pottery

Fire Escape Farms
(online/San Francisco)
Naya@FireEscapeFarms.com
www.fireescapefarms.com

Planters, seeds, tools, accessories for small-spaced gardening

Flora Grubb
1634 Jerrold Avenue
San Francisco
California 94124
(415) 626-7256
www.floragrubb.com

Planted containers, sky planters, wall
ornaments

Gallant and Jones (online/Vancouver)
(604) 420-1350
www.gallantandjones.com
Deckchairs and outdoor furniture

Graceful Gardens
485 Driggs Avenue
Brooklyn
New York 11211
(718) 782-1365
www.gracefulgardensnyc.com

Flowers, terrariums, garden accessories

Grdn
103 Hoyt Street
Brooklyn
New York 11217
(718) 797-3628
www.grdnbklyn.com

A complete shop for the urban gardener

Jayson Home
1885 N Clybourn Avenue
Chicago
Illinois 60614
(800) 472-1885
www.jaysonhome.com

Reclaimed pots and planters, plants,
container planting

Potted
3158 Los Feliz Boulevard
Los Angeles
California 90039
(323) 665-3801
www.pottedstore.com

Bright furniture, water gardens, garden
decorations

Pottery Barn (across USA)
(888) 779-5176
www.potterybarn.com

Outdoor lighting, garden furniture, outdoor
tableware

Pure Modern (online/Canada)
(800) 563-0593
www.puremodern.com
Pots and planters, garden accessories,
contemporary lighting

Rolling Greens
Culver City (310) 559-8656
and Los Angeles (323) 934-4500
www.rollinggreensnursery.com

Plants, containers, vintage furniture,
bird feeders

Sprout Home
Brooklyn (718) 388-4440
and Chicago (312) 226-5950
www.sprouthome.stores.yahoo.net

Contemporary garden accessories,
sustainable furniture, outdoor candles

Sundance Catalog
Utah
(800) 422-2770
www.sundancecatalog.com/home.do

Wooden garden furniture, glass tableware

West Elm (across USA)
(888) 922-4119
www.westelm.com

Outdoor furniture, garden cushions,
umbrella

acknowledgments

Many, many thanks to Debbie Patterson for creating such beautiful images, coming up
with lovely ideas, providing wonderful props, and for generally being such great fun!
Thank you to Gillian Haslam for tremendous support and guidance, and understanding
the need to tidy your stationery drawer when you are supposed to be writing, to Caroline
West for being a pleasure to work with and for making the editing such a painless and
speedy process, and to Geoff Borin for designing the book so beautifully. Thank you to
Sally Powell at Cico for organizing great locations and to Cindy Richards, who gave me the
opportunity to do my first gardening book. Thank you to Chloe Dahl for invaluable help
and woodworking skills! And thank you to Laurie, Gracie, and Betty, for enthusiasm,
ideas, creativity, and everything else.

index